C000276579

POCKET PRAYERS
PRAYERS
FOR ADVENT
AND CHRISTMAS

Other books in the series:

Pocket Prayers Classic Collection
compiled by Christopher Herbert

Pocket Celtic Prayers
compiled by Martin Wallace

Pocket Graces
compiled by Pam Robertson

Pocket Prayers for Children
compiled by Christopher Herbert

Pocket Prayers for Commuters
compiled by Christopher Herbert

Pocket Prayers for Healing and Wholeness
compiled by Trevor Lloyd

Pocket Prayers for Marriage
compiled by Andrew and Pippa Body

Pocket Prayers for Parents
compiled by Hamish and Sue Bruce

Pocket Prayers for Troubled Times
compiled by John Pritchard

Pocket Words of Comfort
compiled by Christopher Herbert

POCKET PRAYERS
FOR ADVENT
AND CHRISTMAS

COMPILED BY
JAN MCFARLANE

CHURCH HOUSE
PUBLISHING

Church House Publishing
Church House
Great Smith Street
London SW1P 3AZ

ISBN 978 0 7151 4196 0

Published 2009 by Church House Publishing

Introduction and compilation copyright © Jan McFarlane 2009

All rights reserved. No part of this publication may be reproduced or
stored or transmitted by any means or in any form, electronic or
mechanical, including photocopying, recording, or any information
storage and retrieval system without written permission, which should
be sought from the Copyright Administrator, Church House Publishing,
Church House, Great Smith Street, London SW1P 3AZ.
Email: copyright@c-of-e.org.uk

The opinions expressed in this book are those of the author and do not
necessarily reflect the official policy of the General Synod or The
Archbishops' Council of the Church of England.

Designed by www.penguinboy.net
Printed in England by Ashford Colour Press Ltd, Fareham, Hants

CONTENTS

Introduction   viii

Waiting . . . the season of Advent   1

Expecting . . . anticipating Christmas Eve   20

Welcoming . . . the miracle of Christmas   31

Celebrating . . . the season of Christmas   40

Journeying . . . New Year and Epiphany   66

Index of first lines   85

Index of authors and sources   90

Acknowledgements   94

The holly bears a berry
as red as any blood;
and Mary bore sweet Jesus Christ
to do poor sinners good.

INTRODUCTION

The run-up to Christmas is busy, busy, busy. All those
presents to buy and wrap; the mince pies to bake; the
Christmas tree lights to disentangle; the nativity
costumes to make. And yet, deep down, we know that
there is more to it than this.

Christmas carols sing to us over the radio and echo in
our hearts, a rich tradition, reminding us of something
we learned long ago; reminding us of a birth,
shepherds, a star and angels. If we can but find a
moment to pause, to reflect, our hectic preparations
can find a new meaning. We're preparing to welcome
God, born in a manger, born for us. This is the greatest
gift of all. The rest is just wrapping.

The aim of this little book is to help us to carve out
that moment to ponder. It's pocket sized to slip easily
into a jacket pocket, a briefcase, a shopping bag. That
moment on the commuter train, that break for a cup
of tea in the middle of the shopping frenzy, the quiet
before bed when the house is still and everyone sleeps
– these can be moments of rest and renewal, of

comfort and challenge. God-with-us. What might that mean for us today?

Each of the five chapters has its own emphasis and theme.

Waiting – covers the season of Advent. Advent Sunday falls at the end of November and gives us four weeks to prepare for Christmas. Perhaps this is the hardest time of all in which to carve out moments to think and pray, but if we can, our efforts will be rewarded and our Christmas celebrations will be all the richer. This chapter contains a prayer a day for the first three weeks of Advent. Each week begins on a Sunday and offers food for thought to nourish us in our busyness. The emphasis is on our preparations to greet the Christmas child, but there are echoes too of the time when we will welcome Christ again – not as a helpless baby born in a manger, but as the King of the universe, at the end of time coming in power to judge the world.

Expecting – steps up a gear and gives us material for contemplation in the final few days before Christmas. We think of Mary waiting to give birth, pondering in her heart the mystery surrounding her child, the promises of the angel. The ancient Advent Antiphons surround the last seven days of Advent with strange imagery – hinting at all that the Christ child will be. Unfamiliar images, they call out for our attention and whet our appetite to learn more about the longed-for promised Messiah and the stories that foretell his birth.

Welcoming – the miracle that is Christmas. This chapter aims to capture the magic of Christmas Eve, the stillness of the midnight hour, the silence before the storm of the celebrations the following day. The weeks of preparation are finally over and we silently welcome a tiny child who will change the course of history. And who can change the course of our lives too.

Celebrating – let the bells ring out – it's Christmas! Bells, carols, incense, presents, crackers, celebrations. We've prepared long and hard and now we relax and rejoice in the birth of a long-expected baby. In the middle of our celebrations we call to mind those for whom Christmas is a difficult time – the bereaved, the broken families, the depressed and ill. We remember that they are the ones to whom Jesus ministers first. And he calls us to do the same.

Journeying – we never stand still for long. The New Year beckons us on and invites us to resolve to do better in the light of all we have learned from the Christmas story. The wise men travel on to Bethlehem with their gifts and call us to offer all that we have in the service of this tiny, life-changing king. We step out into the future with the Light of the World as our guide, ready for all the challenges and opportunities that lie ahead.

HOW TO USE THIS BOOK

For those who like structure, the first chapter offers a prayer a day for the first three weeks of Advent. The second chapter has prayers for the fourth week of Advent, and a prayer a day for the seven days covered by the Advent Antiphons (17–23 December). The third and fourth chapters give a wealth of material to take us from Christmas Eve to New Year's Eve. The final chapter offers a prayer a day from New Year's Eve until the feast of the Epiphany on 6 January, followed by prayers to ponder until the season ends on 2 February.

Please don't feel bound by the structure. Many of us lead gently chaotic lives and we may find that days go by when we are simply too busy or tired to offer more than a brief arrow prayer to God. Don't feel guilty. God understands. But there may suddenly be a moment when the train is delayed or the children's nativity rehearsal overruns. These are golden opportunities to find a prayer that resonates and to read it slowly, perhaps several times, letting the imagery unfold and allowing God to speak to us wherever we are. If we allow him to speak, he will. We simply need to listen.

Jan McFarlane

WAITING...
THE SEASON
OF ADVENT

We're not very good at waiting. If you need evidence, see how early the mince pies arrive on the supermarket shelves. Some supermarkets now stock them all year round. Why? Because we don't want to wait for Christmas.

And yet the season of Advent – the four weeks leading up to Christmas Eve – is all about waiting. And watching. And reflecting. Amid the frantic shopping and the laden lists and the parties and the present wrapping, we're asked to pause for a moment to think. We're asked to prepare ourselves, not just practically but spiritually, to welcome the new-born Christ child.

We're asked to look past the outward trappings of the preparations for Christmas – to look at ourselves, our own lives. And to see them in the light of the God who is to be born in a messy stable, turning all our values upside down. And the God who will come again at the end of time to ask us how we did.

1

THE FIRST WEEK OF ADVENT

The Collect for Advent Sunday

Almighty God,
give us grace that we may cast away
the works of darkness,
and put upon us the armour of light,
now in the time of this mortal life,
in which thy Son Jesus Christ
came to visit us in great humility;
that in the last day,
when he shall come again in his glorious Majesty
to judge both the quick and the dead,
we may rise to the life immortal,
through him who liveth and reigneth
with thee and the Holy Ghost,
now and ever. Amen.

The Book of Common Prayer

Lo, he comes with clouds descending,
once for favoured sinners slain;
thousand thousand saints attending
swell the triumph of his train:
Alleluia!
God appears on earth to reign.

Yea, Amen, let all adore thee,
high on thy eternal throne;
Saviour, take the power and glory,
claim the kingdom for thine own:
Alleluia!
Thou shalt reign, and thou alone.

**Charles Wesley (1707–88) and
John Cennick (1718–55)**

Our heavenly Father,
as once again we prepare for Christmas,
help us to find time in our busy lives
for quiet thought and prayer;
that we may reflect upon the wonder of your love
and allow the story of the Saviour's birth
to penetrate our hearts and minds.
So may our joy be deeper,
our worship more real,
and our lives worthier of all that you have done for us
through the coming of your Son,
Jesus Christ our Lord. Amen.
Frank Colquhoun (1909–97)

God of Abraham and Sarah
and all the patriarchs of old,
you are our Father too.
Your love is revealed to us in Jesus Christ,
Son of God and Son of David.
Help us in preparing to celebrate his birth
to make our hearts ready for your Holy Spirit
to make his home among us.
We ask this through Jesus Christ,
the light who is coming into the world. Amen.
Common Worship: Times and Seasons

Heavenly Father, you have created a universe of light:
forgive us when we return to darkness.
Lord, have mercy.

Lord Jesus, you are the light of the world:
cleanse and heal our blinded sight.
Christ, have mercy.

Holy Spirit, you give us light in our hearts:
renew us in faith and love.
Lord, have mercy.
Common Worship: Times and Seasons

You keep us waiting.
You, the God of all time,
want us to wait
for the right time in which to discover
who we are, where we must go,
who will be with us, and what we must do.
So thank you . . . for the waiting time.
Iona Community Worship Book

Lord,
I turn my thoughts
to you.

Within the whirlwind of my day
I stop
and think of you.

It's far too easy to forget you
in the busyness and bustle
of the day,
as other pressures crowd and fill my mind.
And when I pause
I find myself
astonished
that whilst your closeness has been crowded out
yet still
you have been there,
your steady love surrounding me.

Hello again, Lord.
Pat Marsh

THE SECOND WEEK OF ADVENT

God our Father,
you spoke to the prophets of old
of a Saviour who would bring peace.
You helped them to spread the joyful message
of his coming kingdom.
Help us, as we prepare to celebrate his birth,
to share with those around us
the good news of your power and love.
We ask this through Jesus Christ,
the light who is coming into the world. Amen.

Common Worship: Times and Seasons

We are brighter than a thousand suns,
cleverer than two thousand years,
all power belongs to us,
except the power to make peace:
except that there is an ancient darkness of our hearts
and a rage that steals our sanity.
God forgive us
and let true light shine on us
and your world.

Bob Warwicker

With love and compassion,
come, Lord Jesus.
With judgement and mercy,
come, Lord Jesus.
In power and glory,
come, Lord Jesus.
In wisdom and truth,
come, Lord Jesus.

Common Worship: Times and Seasons

For the darkness of waiting
of not knowing what is to come
of staying ready and quiet and attentive,
we praise you O God:
For the darkness and the light
are both alike to you.

For the darkness of staying silent
for the terror of having nothing to say
and for the greater terror
of needing to say nothing,
we praise you O God:
For the darkness and the light
are both alike to you.

For the darkness of loving
in which it is safe to surrender
to let go of our self-protection
and to stop holding back our desire,
we praise you O God:
For the darkness and the light
are both alike to you.

For the darkness of choosing
when you give us the moment
to speak, and act, and change,
and we cannot know what we have set in motion,
but we still have to take the risk,
we praise you O God:
For the darkness and the light
are both alike to you.

For the darkness of hoping
in a world which longs for you,
for the wrestling and the labouring of all creation
for wholeness and justice and freedom,
we praise you O God:
For the darkness and the light
are both alike to you.

Janet Morley

Lord Jesus Christ,
your world awaits you.
In the longing of the persecuted for justice;
in the longing of the poor for prosperity;
in the longing of the privileged
for riches greater than wealth;
in the longing of our hearts for a better life;
and in the song of your Church,
expectation is ever present.

O come, Lord, desire behind our greatest needs.
O come, Lord, liberator of humanity.
O come, Lord, O come, Immanuel. Amen.
Book of Common Order of the Church of Scotland

The night is far spent, and the day is at hand:
let us therefore cast off the works of darkness,
and let us put on the armour of light.
Romans 13.12 AV

At the setting of the sun,
in the enveloping darkness of night,
at the interplay of hours
with sunlight giving way to moonlight,
I step from the day into the night
with a desire to be still,
and in being still
to turn to you, O God,
and in turning to you
to return to the creative depths of my soul.

At the setting of the sun,
in the darkness of the night
I turn to you.

J. Philip Newell

THE THIRD WEEK OF ADVENT

God our Father,
you gave to Zechariah and Elizabeth in their old age
a son called John.
He grew up strong in spirit,
prepared the people for the coming of the Lord,
and baptized them in the Jordan
to wash away their sins.
Help us, who have been baptized into Christ,
to be ready to welcome him into our hearts,
and to grow strong in faith by the power of the Spirit.
We ask this through Jesus Christ,
the light who is coming into the world. Amen.

Common Worship: Times and Seasons

God of the watching ones,
the waiting ones,
the slow and suffering ones,
the angels in heaven,
the child in the womb,
give us your benediction,
your good word for our souls,
that we might rest and rise
in the kindness of your company. Amen.

Cloth for the Cradle

Lord,
it is night.

The night is for stillness.
Let us be still in the presence of God.

It is night after a long day.
What has been done has been done;
what has not been done has not been done;
let it be.

The night is dark.
Let our fears of the darkness of the world
and of our own lives
rest in you.

The night is quiet.
Let the quietness of your peace enfold us,
all dear to us,
and all who have no peace.

The night heralds the dawn.
Let us look expectantly to a new day,
new joys, new possibilities.

In your name we pray. Amen.
Vows and Partings

Stop, my child.
Stop rushing for a moment.

Put down the complex heavy baggage of your life.
Release your weary grip
upon the endless struggles which you battle with
and try to hide behind.

Dare to let go for a moment
and dare to walk away.

Take time.
   Relax.
     Be still.
       Immerse yourself in stillness.

Drink deeply of the silence
and feel
the pulsing heartbeat of your God.

Awaken your soul
to mystery;
reaffirm
the profound simplicity of his love.

Let the intimacy of his love

tenderly embrace you.

Let the warmth of his love
gently nurture you.

Let the joy of his love
enrich you.

Dwell on him in your heart
    and know
      that he
        is less than a whisper away.

Pat Marsh

Lord Jesus, light of the world,
blessed is Gabriel, who brought good news;
blessed is Mary, your mother and ours.
Bless your Church preparing for Christmas;
and bless us your children, who long for your coming.
Amen.

Common Worship: Times and Seasons

Jesus, who came to earth as a helpless baby;
Jesus, the lamb of God born in a stable;
Jesus, the Prince of Peace who slept on hay;
Jesus, whose birth caused the angels to sing;
Jesus, whose glory lit up the sky;
Jesus, whose coming was foretold;
Jesus, who gave us his life;
Jesus, who draws us with love;
Jesus, our Saviour, our King:
come, Lord Jesus, come. Amen.

Michael Perry (1942–96) with
Patrick Goodland and Angela Griffiths

O eternal Light
shine into our hearts.
O eternal Goodness
deliver us from evil.
O eternal Power
be our strength.
O eternal Wisdom
dispel the darkness of our ignorance.
O eternal Pity
show mercy on us.
Grant that we may ever seek your countenance
with all our heart, mind and strength.
And in your infinite mercy
enable us to reach your holy presence. Amen.

Alcuin (c. 735–804)

expecting...
ANTICIPATING CHRISTMAS eve

Christmas is nearly upon us. The sense of panic mounts. Are the presents bought and wrapped? Is the turkey going to fit in the oven? How can the children's sheep costumes for the Nativity look more 'sheep' and less 'glue stick and cotton wool'?

And yet, if we will allow, the sense of mystery deepens. The quiet anticipation of the birth of the Christ child grows inside us, the expectation bubbling and rising.

The childlike excitement of Christmas Day can revisit us as adults as we wait with bated breath for the first cry of the new-born Son of God.

THE FOURTH WEEK OF ADVENT

God our redeemer,
who didst prepare the Blessed Virgin Mary
to be the mother of thy Son:
grant that, as she looked for his coming as our saviour,
so we may be ready to greet him
when he shall come again to be our judge;
who liveth and reigneth with thee
in the unity of the Holy Spirit,
one God, now and for ever. Amen.

Common Worship

Loving God,
calling your friends in new and unexpected ways,
choosing Mary from the powerless and unnoticed in
the world,
yet greatly loved and cherished in your sight,
that she should be the mother of our Saviour;
so fill us with your grace
that we too may accept the promptings of your Spirit,
and welcome your angel with glad and open arms,
ready to be pierced with pain and filled with joy,
rejoicing in the cost of your salvation,
in and through the same Jesus our Messiah. Amen.

Jim Cotter

Mary the slumdweller
Mary, who longed for the liberation of her people
Mary, who sang to the God of the poor
Mary, homeless in Bethlehem
Mother of the longed-for Saviour
Mary, exiled from her native land
Mary, pilgrim with her people
Blessed are you among women.

Noticias Aliadas

And thou, Jesus, sweet Lord,
art thou not also a mother?
Truly thou art a mother,
the mother of all mothers,
who tasted death,
in thy desire to give life to thy children.

Anselm (c. 1033–1109)

In the silence before time began,
in the quiet of the womb,
in the stillness of early morning
is your beauty.
At the heart of all creation,
at the birth of every creature,
at the centre of each moment
is your splendour.
Rekindle in me the sparks of your beauty
that I may be part of the splendour of this moment.
Rekindle in me the sparks of your beauty
that I may be part of the blazing splendour
that burns from the heart of this moment.

J. Philip Newell

I never, O God,
want to live in complacent sloth,
soggy in religious routine,
smug in pious satisfaction.
I want to be expectant
and ready for the new thing that you are doing today,
and again tomorrow. Amen.

Eugene H. Peterson

THE ADVENT ANTIPHONS

Perhaps one of the best loved of the Advent hymns is the haunting and evocative 'O come, O come, Emmanuel'. Its roots lie in a series of short Latin verses that date back to the seventh century and which were used in worship in the seven days leading up to Christmas Eve. These 'Advent Antiphons' have been handed down from generation to generation and are used in our worship today. Their strange but powerful imagery causes us to stop and think. This Jesus, when he comes, what will he be like? We need to spend time with the antiphons – pondering them, playing with the curious images, letting them speak to our imagination. Our sense of anticipation deepens.

O come, O come, Emmanuel,
and ransom captive Israel,
that mourns in lonely exile here,
until the Son of God appear:
Rejoice! rejoice! Emmanuel
shall come to thee, O Israel.
John Mason Neale (trans.) (1818–66)

17 December – *O Sapientia*

O *Wisdom*, coming forth from the Most High
filling all creation
and reigning to the ends of the earth;
come and teach us the way of truth.
Amen. Come, Lord Jesus.

The Promise of His Glory

18 December – *O Adonai*

O *Lord* of Israel, ruler of your ancient people,
you appeared to Moses in the burning bush
and gave the law on Mount Sinai:
Come and reach out your hand to save us.

Western Rite adapted by Angela Ashwin

19 December – *O Radix Jesse*

A green Shoot will sprout from *Jesse's* stump,*
from his roots a budding *Branch*.
The life-giving Spirit of GOD will hover over him,
the Spirit that brings wisdom and understanding,
the Spirit that gives direction and builds strength,
the Spirit that instills knowledge and Fear-of-GOD.
Fear-of-GOD
will be all his joy and delight.

He won't judge by appearances,
won't decide on the basis of hearsay.
He'll judge the needy by what is right,
render decisions on earth's poor with justice.
His words will bring everyone to awed attention.
A mere breath from his lips will topple the wicked.
Each morning he'll pull on sturdy work clothes and
boots,
and build righteousness and faithfulness in the land.
Isaiah 11.1-5, THE MESSAGE

**Jesse was the father of King David. The promised Messiah
was to be 'of David's line'. Jesus' roots can be traced
through the family tree back to King David, and his father
Jesse.*

20 December – *O Clavis David*
O come, O come, thou *David's key*,
unlock the gate and set us free.
Descendent of the king of old,
release us from oppression's hold.
Rejoice! Rejoice! in words that sing
true liberty shall soon take wing.
  Jim Cotter

21 December – *O Oriens*

Christ is the *morning star*
who, when the night of this world is passed,
brings to his saints
the promise of the light of life
and opens everlasting day.
The Venerable Bede (673–735)

22 December – *O Rex Gentium*

Thy kingdom come, O God,
thy rule, O Christ, begin;
break with thine iron rod
the tyrannies of sin.

When comes the promised time
that war shall be no more,
and lust, oppression, crime
shall flee thy face before?

O'er lands both near and far
thick darkness broodeth yet:
arise, O Morning Star,
arise and never set!
Lewis Hensley (1824–1905)

23 December – *O Emmanuel*

O come, O come, Emmanuel,
God-with-us here and now to dwell,
at one with our humanity,
in whom we find our destiny.
    Rejoice! Rejoice! The human face
    of God with us shall interlace.

Jim Cotter

Christmas Eve

Come, thou long-expected Jesus,
born to set thy people free;
from our fears and sins release us;
let us find our rest in thee.

Born thy people to deliver;
born a child and yet a king;
born to reign in us for ever;
now thy gracious kingdom bring.

Charles Wesley (1707–88)

A prayer before a carol service

Lord, we have sung these carols and heard this story
so many times before.
We confess that we have allowed
the most important event in history
to become dulled by familiarity.
Come to us in this act of worship
and capture our minds with truth.
May we see the Creator of the universe
in a newborn child.
May we worship him with joy. Amen.

John Searle

WELCOMING...
THE
MIRACLE OF
CHRISTMAS

'How silently, how silently the wondrous gift is given.'
Midnight Mass is one of the best attended services in the
Church's year. It's not surprising. When all the
preparations for Christmas have finally been made, the
over-excited children are finally asleep, and what isn't done
now will never get done, we can at last draw breath. In the
silence of the midnight hour, we welcome in our new-born
King.

There is something special about the silence of midnight.
It's a moment to pause in wonder at the crib. To be held
transfixed by the miracle of this birth before which all the
tinsel and trimmings fade into insignificance. Here is the
greatest gift of all – a gift no money can buy. God is with
us. Alleluia!

How silently, how silently,
the wondrous gift is given!
so God imparts to human hearts
the blessings of his heaven.
No ear may hear his coming;
but in this world of sin,
where meek souls will receive him, still
the dear Christ enters in.

Phillips Brooks (1835–93)

Eternal God,
who made this most holy night
to shine with the brightness of your one true light:
bring us, who have known the revelation of that life
on earth,
to see the radiance of your heavenly glory;
through Jesus Christ your Son our Lord,
who is alive and reigns with you,
in the unity of the Holy Spirit,
one God, now and for ever. Amen.

Common Worship: Times and Seasons

Welcome all wonders in one sight!
Eternity shut in a span.
Summer in winter, day in night,
heaven in earth and God in man.

Great little one whose all-embracing birth
brings earth to heaven, stoops heaven to earth.
Richard Crashaw (1613–49)

Let all mortal flesh keep silence
and with fear and trembling stand;
ponder nothing earthly-minded,
for with blessing in his hand
Christ our God to earth descendeth,
our full homage to demand.
From the Liturgy of St James
Gerard Moultrie (trans.)(1829–85)

Who is this, whose human birth
here proclaims him child of earth?
He it is who formed the skies,
saw the new-made stars arise:
life immortal, light divine,
blinking in the candle-shine;
born our darkness to dispel,
God with us, Emmanuel!
Timothy Dudley-Smith

Silent night, holy night:
Son of God, love's pure light
radiant beams from thy holy face,
with the dawn of redeeming grace,
Jesus, Lord, at thy birth.
Joseph Mohr (1792–1848)
John F. Young (trans.) (1820–85)

Lord Jesus Christ,
your birth at Bethlehem
draws us to kneel in wonder at heaven touching earth:
accept our heartfelt praise
as we worship you,
our Saviour and our eternal God. Amen.
Common Worship: Times and Seasons

Since you so graciously invite us
to yourself, Almighty God,
do not withdraw the invitation
however deaf we remain.
Grant that I may be disciplined
and open to your word,
obeying you, not just for a single day,
nor yet a few weeks,
but to the end of my life,
for the sake of Jesus Christ our Lord. Amen.

John Calvin (1509–64)

What can we bring to your sufficiency
but our poverty?
What can we bring to your beauty
but our wretchedness?
What can we bring to your wholeness
but our woundedness?

Made poor, wretched and wounded for our sakes,
you welcome us, wherever we are,
whatever we bring.

Kate Compston

Today, O God,
the soles of your feet
have touched the earth.
Today,
the back street, the forgotten place
have been lit up with significance.
Today,
the households of earth
welcome the King of heaven.
For you have come among us,
you are one of us.
So may our songs rise to surround your throne
as our knees bend to salute your cradle. Amen.
Book of Common Order of the Church of Scotland

God, of your goodness
give me yourself
for only in you
have I all.

Julian of Norwich (c. 1342–1413)

Cradled in the mystery
that where I stand
is holy ground,
I rest
in awe.

Embraced
in the truth
that he who loves me
with a love beyond all knowing
is both with me
and within me
in this place,
I rest
in the joy
of being deeply blessed.

He
is in me
and I in him.

What mystery . . .

What precious holy ground . . .

What a gift.
Pat Marsh

Light looked down and beheld Darkness;
'Thither will I go,' said Light.
Peace looked down and beheld War.
'Thither will I go,' said Peace.
Love looked down and beheld Hatred.
'Thither will I go,' said Love.
So came Light, and shone;
So came Peace, and gave rest;
So came Love, and brought life.
And the Word was made Flesh, and dwelt among us.

Laurence Housman (1865–1959)

And the Word became flesh and lived among us,
and we have seen his glory,
the glory as of a father's only son,
full of grace and truth.

John 1.14, NRSV

Yea, Lord, we greet thee,
born this happy morning,
Jesu, to thee be glory given;
Word of the Father,
now in flesh appearing:
O come, let us adore him,
Christ the Lord!

Latin, eighteenth century
Frederick Oakeley (1802–80) and others (trans.)

CELEBRATING
...THE
SEASON OF
CHRISTMAS

'O come, let us adore him, Christ the Lord!' Christmas Day – a day for celebration! Thoughtful presents exchanged remind us of the gifts the wise men will bring to the baby Jesus at Epiphany. An abundance of good food and fine wine – signs and symbols of God's lavish creation – and, replete, we snooze before the fire. Tomorrow the sales will begin in town, hinting that Christmas is over – business back to usual – but for the Church it's only just begun!

The carols, which shouldn't really be sung before Christmas Eve, will continue to resound for the full forty days of Christmas. The tree may come down by twelfth night – but the crib can stay in place until the Feast of the Presentation on 2 February. We've prepared long and hard for this – let's not hurry our celebrations.

But we're not allowed to stay too long, gazing at our new-born king. Babies are magnetic – hours can be spent simply watching them, absorbed in awe of the miracle of new life. But the Christmas child is born for a purpose. He has a job to do. The day after Christmas the Church remembers Stephen, the first of the followers of Jesus to lose his life for his faith. We remember the 'Holy Innocents' – the young children slaughtered by King Herod in a fit of jealous rage and fear that his kingdom was at threat. We remember those for whom Christmas is a difficult and painful time.

This baby has a broken, pain-filled world to heal. And he needs our help.

In the beginning was the Word,
and the Word was with God,
and the Word was God.
John 1.1, NRSV

Almighty God,
you have given us your only-begotten Son
to take our nature upon him
and as at this time to be born of a pure virgin:
grant that we, who have been born again
and made your children by adoption and grace,
may daily be renewed by your Holy Spirit;
through Jesus Christ your Son our Lord. Amen.
Common Worship: Times and Seasons

Christians, awake! salute the happy morn,
whereon the Saviour of the world was born;
rise to adore the mystery of love,
which hosts of angels chanted from above:
with them the joyful tidings first begun
of God incarnate and the Virgin's Son.
John Byrom (1692–1763)

Loving God,
we give you thanks for the shepherds in the fields
who so gladly heard and responded
to the news of the birth of the Saviour.
Keep us honest and industrious in doing our work;
keep us alert, ready to hear your messengers;
make us eager and active in responding to your word;
give us faithfulness in sharing the good news with
others;
fill us with joy in our meeting with the Christ-child.
May our praise and worship be offered for your glory.
Amen.

John Johansan-Berg

Hark! the herald angels sing
glory to the new-born King,
peace on earth and mercy mild,
God and sinners reconciled.
Joyful, all ye nations rise,
join the triumph of the skies;
with the angelic host proclaim,
'Christ is born in Bethlehem.'
Hark, the herald angels sing
glory to the new-born King.

Charles Wesley (1707–88)

O God the Son, highest and holiest,
who humbled yourself to share our birth
and our death:
bring us with the shepherds and the wise men
to kneel before your holy cradle,
that we may come to sing with your angels
your glorious praises in heaven;
where with the Father and the Holy Spirit
you live and reign,
God, world without end. Amen.

Common Worship: Times and Seasons

I danced in the morning
when the world was begun,
And I danced in the moon
and the stars and the sun,
and I came down from heaven
and I danced on the earth;
at Bethlehem
I had my birth:

Dance, then, wherever you may be;
I am the Lord of the Dance, said he,
and I'll lead you all, wherever you may be,
and I'll lead you all in the dance, said he.
Sydney Carter (1915–2004)

Glorious and forgiving king of heaven:
on your people have mercy.
You whom the cherubim praise:
on your people have mercy.
You whom the seraphim adore:
on your people have mercy.
Christ enthroned in heaven,
praised by the ninefold choir of angels:
on your people have mercy.
Christ worshipped by the Church
throughout the world,
and to whom the whole creation offers its praise:
on your people have mercy.
Christ whom the saints in glory delight to honour:
on your people have mercy.
Lord Jesus, gentle son of Mary,
Redeemer of the world:
on your people have mercy.
Son of God, neither made nor created
but begotten of the Father by the Holy Spirit:
on your people have mercy.
Son of Righteousness, in unclouded glory,
who will come to judge the living and the dead:
on your people have mercy.

St Dunstan (c. 909–88)

Of the Father's heart begotten
Ere the world from chaos rose,
He is Alpha: from that Fountain,
All that is and hath been flows;
He is Omega, of all things
Yet to come the mystic Close,
Evermore and evermore.

Sing, ye heights of heaven, his praises;
Angels and Archangels, sing!
Wheresoe'er ye be, ye faithful,
Let your joyous anthems ring,
Every tongue his name confessing,
Countless voices answering,
Evermore and evermore.

Prudentius (348–c. 413)
John Mason Neale (trans.)(1818–66)

PRAYERS BEFORE THE CHRISTMAS CRIB

I open the stable door;
I kneel before the infant;
I worship with the shepherds;
I adore the Christ child.
I give my love with Mary and Joseph;
I wonder at the 'Word made flesh',
I am aware of the love of God;
I sing glory with the angels;
I offer my gifts with the wise men.
I receive the living Lord;
I hold him in my hands;
I go on my way rejoicing,
glorifying and praising God.

David Adam

Little Lamb, who made thee?
Dost thou know who made thee?
Gave thee life and bid thee feed.
by the stream and o'er the mead;
gave thee clothing of delight,
softest clothing, woolly, bright;
gave thee such a tender voice
making all the vales rejoice:
Little Lamb, who made thee?
Dost thou know who made thee?

Little Lamb, I'll tell thee,
Little Lamb, I'll tell thee;
He is called by thy name,
For he calls himself a Lamb:
He is meek and he is mild,
he became a little child.
I a child, and thou a lamb,
We are called by his name,
Little Lamb, God bless thee,
Little Lamb, God bless thee.

William Blake (1757–1827)

Jesus, good above all other,
gentle child of gentle mother,
in a stable born our brother,
give us grace to persevere.
Percy Dearmer (1867–1936)

Nativity Child,
awaken anew the child in me.

By the light of the star
which heralded your birth
light up my life with your joy.

Give me the capacity to see
as a little child sees;
the ability to see the precious jewels
hidden in the everyday moment.
Help me to see with eyes that look upon the world
in simple wide-eyed wonder.

As a young child offers its hand
into the warmth and reassurance
of its father's,
help me to trust in you.

Like a peaceful child,
tenderly cuddled on its father's lap,
help me to nestle snugly
into the warm embrace of your loving arms.

Help me to celebrate the name
of the Nativity Child
with all the boisterous exuberance of a toddler.
Help me to dance, to sing, to skip,
to simply splash around
in the delight of your love.

As I stride out,
wander off like a little child,
help me to know your eyes are ever on me,
lovingly, tenderly watching me,
protecting me from harm.

And should I fall, Lord,
gently pick me up.

Nativity Child,
awaken anew the child in me,
that in simple trust and wide-eyed wonder
I may let you lead me
into being that which I was born to be.

Pat Marsh

Blessed art thou,
O Christmas Christ,
that thy cradle was so low
that shepherds,
poorest and simplest of earthly folk,
could yet kneel beside it,
and look level-eyed into the face of God.
Author unknown

In my mother's womb
you knew me, O God.
In my father's birth
and in the birth of his father
were my beginnings.
At the inception of time
and even before time began
your love conceived of my being.
As you have known me
so may I come to know you.
As you prepared my birth
so may I make way for fresh birthings of your Spirit.
As you sowed all things in love
so may your love for all things be born in me,
so may your love be born again in me.
J. Philip Newell

Helpless God as child and crucified,
laid in a cradle and cradled on a cross;
help us discern in your submission
not weakness but the passionate work of love.

Michael H. Taylor

Born in the night,
Mary's Child,
A long way from your home;
coming in need,
Mary's Child,
born in a borrowed room.

Clear shining light,
Mary's Child,
your face lights up our way;
Light of the world,
Mary's Child,
dawn on our darkened day.

Truth of our life,
Mary's Child,
you tell us God is good;
prove it is true,
Mary's Child,
go to your cross of wood.

Hope of the world,
Mary's Child,
You're coming soon to reign;
King of the earth,
Mary's Child,
walk in our streets again.

Geoffrey Ainger

AND FOR THOSE WHO CANNOT CELEBRATE...

God of hope,
when every minute seems like an hour,
when days are empty and bleak,
when nights are lonely and long,
when the ache inside does not fade
help me to find peace and comfort
in the encircling of your arms. Amen.

Vows and Partings

Lord,
there is much in my mind that has healed,
but still there is pain in my heart.
I do not always feel forgiving or forgiven:
wounds still hurt and doubts remain.

I prefer a life with no remainders
and situations with no loose ends.

Help me to understand that life is not like that.

May I find the place in my life where I can move on,
where I can be cleansed from previous bitterness,
and where I can be set free from recurring passions
that torment my spirit. Amen.
Vows and Partings

God of grace,
in my rejection I remember
the cruel words which all too easily
undermine my confidence;
the harsh actions which make me feel worthless;
the petty complaints which make me feel useless,
and the scornful looks which make me feel
unloved and unlovable.
Help me to know that I am your child,
of infinite worth,
both loved and loveable. Amen.

Vows and Partings

God our Father,
you sent your Son full of grace and truth:
forgive our failure to receive him.
Lord, have mercy.

Jesus our Saviour,
you were born in poverty and laid in a manger:
forgive our greed and rejection of your ways.
Christ, have mercy.

Spirit of love,
your servant Mary responded joyfully to your call:
forgive the hardness of our hearts.
Lord, have mercy.

Common Worship: Times and Seasons

26 DECEMBER – ST STEPHEN

Gracious Father,
who gavest to the first martyr Stephen
grace to pray for those who took up stones against
him:
grant that in all our sufferings for the truth
we may learn to love even our enemies
and to seek forgiveness for those who desire our hurt,
looking up to heaven to him who was crucified for us,
Jesus Christ, our mediator and advocate,
who liveth and reigneth with thee
in the unity of the Holy Spirit,
one God, now and for ever. Amen.

Common Worship

27 DECEMBER – ST JOHN THE EVANGELIST

From the very first day we were there, taking it all in –
we heard it with our own ears,
saw it with our own eyes,
verified it with our own hands.
The Word of Life appeared right before our eyes,
we saw it happen!
And now we're telling you in most sober prose
that what we witnessed was, incredibly, this:
The infinite Life of God himself
took shape before us.

We saw it, we heard it, and now we're telling you
so you can experience it along with us,
this experience of communion
with the Father and his Son, Jesus Christ.
Our motive for writing is simply this:
We want you to enjoy this, too.
Your joy will double our joy!

1John 1.1-4 THE MESSAGE

28 DECEMBER – THE HOLY INNOCENTS

Why, God?
Why did our child
have to die?

Susan Hardwick

For everyone born, a place at the table,
for everyone born, clean water and bread,
a shelter, a space, a safe place for growing,
for everyone born, a star overhead.

For everyone born, a place at the table,
to live without fear, and simply to be,
to work, to speak out, to witness and worship,
for everyone born, the right to be free.

And God will delight when we are creators
of justice and joy, compassion and peace:
yes, God will delight when we are creators
of justice, justice and joy!

Shirley Erena Murray

Thank you,
scandalous God,
for giving yourself to the world
not in the powerful and extraordinary
but in weakness and the familiar:
in a baby; in bread and wine.

Thank you
for offering, at journey's end, a new beginning;
for setting, in the poverty of a stable,
the richest jewel of your love;
for revealing, in a particular place,
your light for all nations . . .

Thank you
for bringing us to Bethlehem, House of Bread,
where the empty are filled,
and the filled are emptied;
where the poor find riches,
and the rich recognize their poverty;
where all who kneel and hold out their hands
are unstintingly fed.

Kate Compston

Sing high
of Son low
in cattle-crib
and candle glow.
Oh! Glory be!
Some shepherds see
time nestle
in eternity.

Sing low
of Son high,
on grisly cross
against the sky.
At Bethlehem
and Calvary
the finite
finds eternity.

Johnstone G. Patrick

Come on, ye faithful,
and all people of goodwill,
it is time to be midwives
for the love of God
struggling again to birth;
delivering healing
to our crying world.

Ann Lewin from 'Christmas Carol'

JOURNEYING ...NEW YEAR AND EPIPHANY

New Year – a time for new beginnings – the expectant turning of a blank page ready to record our story. Time to resolve what that story will be.

The wise men from the East travel on, following a star, reminding us that we too are on a journey – the journey of life. And the best guide of all is the Light of the World. The feast of the Epiphany on 6 January marks the arrival of the wise men bearing their gifts. Epiphany means 'manifestation' and in this season we see how Jesus is 'manifest' – revealed for who he is. First, his baptism in the river Jordan by his cousin John, with a voice from heaven telling us that this is God's own Son. And then in the first of his miracles, at a wedding in Cana where water is turned into wine – a sign of God's abundance and generous life, which he longs to share with all who will follow him.

And finally our Christmas season comes to a close. We remember that the swaddling cloths of the manger are soon to be replaced by cloths binding a body for burial – and we call to mind the cloths left abandoned in the empty tomb. We turn, set our faces to Jerusalem, and travel on to Easter.

NEW YEAR'S EVE

I said to the man who stood
at the gate of the year:
'Give me a light that I may tread
Safely into the unknown.'
And he replied:
'Go out into the darkness
and put your hand into
the hand of God.
That shall be to you
better than a light
and safer than a known way.'
Minnie Louise Haskins (1875–1957)

NEW YEAR'S DAY

I am no longer my own but yours.
Your will, not mine, be done in all things,
wherever you may place me,
in all that I do and in all that I may endure;
when there is work for me and when there is none;
when I am troubled and when I am at peace.
Your will be done
when I am valued and when I am disregarded;
when I find fulfilment and when it is lacking;
when I have all things and when I have nothing.
I willingly offer all that I have and am
to serve you, as and where you choose.
Glorious and blessed God,
Father, Son and Holy Spirit,
you are mine and I am yours.
May it be so for ever.
Let this covenant now made on earth
be fulfilled in heaven. Amen.

Common Worship: Times and Seasons

Too many people around me, Lord,
think of the future,
when they think of it at all,
with dread.
Taught by you,
I will anticipate it with joy,
knowing that your will is done on earth
as it is in heaven. Amen.

Eugene H. Peterson

We pray for the coming of God's kingdom.

You sent your Son to bring good news to the poor,
sight to the blind,
freedom to the captives
and salvation to your people:
anoint us with your Spirit;
rouse us to work in his name.
Father, by your Spirit bring in your kingdom.

Send us to bring help to the poor
and freedom to the oppressed.
Father, by your Spirit bring in your kingdom.

Send us to tell the world
the good news of your healing love.
Father, by your Spirit bring in your kingdom.

Send us to those who mourn,
to bring joy and gladness instead of grief.
Father, by your Spirit bring in your kingdom.

Send us to proclaim that the time is here
for you to save your people.
Father, by your Spirit bring in your kingdom.

Father, use us, unworthy as we are,
to bring in your kingdom of mercy, justice, love and
peace.
Empower us by your Spirit and unite us in your Son,
that all our joy and delight may be to serve you,
now and for ever. Amen.

New Patterns for Worship

Whatever is happening in this world, Lord,
may I always seek first your glory.
May your splendour fill me with light,
far beyond the splendour
of the sun or moon or shining stars;
may I appreciate the beauty of your kingdom
as revealed in the gospel
and see the brightness of your glory
piercing through the darkness and despair of this
world
towards our eternal inheritance
in Christ Jesus our Lord. Amen.

John Calvin (1509–64)

Help me to go forward,
without wanting to know
what I'm going to find
at every bend on the road,
not with my head in the clouds
but with my feet on the ground
and my hand in yours.

I'll leave home then, Lord,
confidently, joyfully
and I'll set out fearlessly on the unknown road:
the journey of life is before me
but you are travelling with me.

Michel Quoist (1921–97)

THE EPIPHANY

When they saw that the star had stopped,
they were overwhelmed with joy.
On entering the house,
they saw the child with Mary his mother;
and they knelt down and paid him homage.
Then, opening their treasure-chests,
they offered him gifts of gold,
frankincense, and myrrh.

Matthew 2.10–11 NRSV

Creator of the heavens,
who led the Magi by a star
to worship the Christ child;
guide and sustain us,
that we may find our journey's end
in Jesus Christ our Lord. Amen.

Common Worship: Times and Seasons

O worship the Lord in the beauty of holiness;
bow down before him, his glory proclaim;
with gold of obedience, and incense of lowliness,
kneel and adore him: the Lord is his name.

John Samuel Bewley Monsell (1811–75)

God, when I see how kings and nations
slip into shadows at Jesus' birth,
I see that I will do well not to become engrossed
in either of them.
It will not be by excavating Bethlehem
or by analyzing Herod
but by worshipping you
that my life will find centre and purpose. Amen.

Eugene H. Peterson

Be thou a bright flame before me,
Be thou a guiding star above me,
Be thou a smooth path below me,
Be thou a good shepherd behind me,
Today, tonight, and for ever. Amen.

St Columba of Iona (c. 521–97)

Will you come and see the light from the stable door?
It is shining newly bright,
though it shone before.
It will be your guiding star,
it will show you who you are.
Will you hide or decide to meet the light?

Brian Wren

Lord, by the song of the angels
you disclosed your birth to your own people,
and by the leading of a star
you revealed your glory to strangers.
Teach us to know you now
and to make you known to all. Amen.

Common Worship: Times and Seasons

Beckoning God –
who called the rich to travel toward poverty,
the wise to embrace your folly,
the powerful to know their own frailty;
who gave to strangers
a sense of homecoming in an alien land
and to stargazers
true light and vision as they bowed to earth –
we lay ourselves open to your signs for us.

Stir us with holy discontent over a world
which gives its gifts to those
who have plenty already
whose talents are obvious
whose power is recognized;
and help us
both to share our resources with those who have little
and to receive with humility the gifts they bring to us.

Rise within us, like a star,
and make us restless
till we journey forth
to seek our rest in you.

Kate Compston

The wise men were not wise
because they wore big hats,
or held a plan of all the stars,
but because they walked a thousand miles
to see a child.

Such a trek seems madness
to educated lookers-on.
But there the difference lies
between the ones who look
and then the ones who see beyond.

Three wise men came from the east
who knew enough to know
that things are never as they seem.

In the secret of my heart
teach me wisdom.
Donal Neary SJ and Dermot King SJ

The kings, Lord,
brought myrrh, frankincense and gold.
Lord, we have nothing of our own to bring;
we bring you what you have given:
our lives for your life. Amen.

Common Worship: Times and Seasons

Creator God,
you chose representatives from outside Israel
to witness the birth of your Son,
so that all the world would be a part
of that momentous event.
And their gifts of gold, frankincense and myrrh,
as representing different aspects of life,
showed that all life is gathered into your care.
But sometimes your church excludes
both people and parts of life.
Creator God, may we soften the boundaries of your church,
so that nothing and no-one is excluded from your house
save by choice. Amen.

Janice Scott

Stirring the easy slumbers
of my consciousness,
he jolts me
from the cosy rut
I'd channelled for myself.
Breaking the mould of others' expectations,
he questions once more
the status quo in me.
Prompting me to steer my route
across unchartered ground,
he challenges me
to set my feet on pathways new.

It's not an easy option, following God.

For he calls me in directions
where I had not thought to go,
requires of me
a courage which I did not think I had,
turns on their head
my preconceived ideas and plans.

It's not an easy option,
following God.

Pat Marsh

O Lord of light and salvation,
guide us safely in your way,
and help us to be true guides
of all who would follow us. Amen.

David Sheppard (1929–2005) and
Derek Worlock (1920–96)

JESUS' BAPTISM

Baptism
Birth by drowning,
upheaval of a settled way of life.
All birth is dying,
a painful separation from the past.
Our first birth called us from
security, to face the life long
struggle to survive.
Our second, no less vigorously
calls us to set out on our
pilgrimage with Christ,
finding in him, with all our
fellow pilgrims, new insights
into love, and truth and life.
A pilgrimage that daunts us
and excites us
and will not let us rest till
we arrive. Our only certainty
God's promise, 'My love will hold you,
do not be afraid.'

Ann Lewin

May God the Holy Spirit,
who came upon the beloved Son
at his baptism in the river Jordan,
pour out his gifts on you
who have come to the waters of new birth. Amen.
Common Worship: Times and Seasons

THE FIRST MIRACLE

At Cana's wedding, long ago,
they knew his presence by this sign,
a virtue none but Christ could show,
to turn their water into wine:
and still on us his blessing be
as in the days of Galilee.
Timothy Dudley-Smith

Songs of thankfulness and praise,
Jesu, Lord, to thee we raise,
manifested by the star
to the stages from afar;
branch of royal David's stem
in thy birth at Bethlehem:
anthems be to thee addrest,
God in man made manifest.

Manifest at Jordan's stream,
Prophet, Priest, and King supreme;
and at Cana, wedding-guest
in thy Godhead manifest;
manifest in power divine,
changing water into wine:
anthems be to thee addrest,
God in man made manifest.

Christopher Wordsworth (1807–85)

2 FEBRUARY – CANDLEMAS

May the light of God illumine your path;
May Christ, the light of the world,
make your life radiant;
May the star of the Spirit
make the night as bright as the day for you;
May Father, Son and Spirit illumine your pilgrim way.
Amen.

John Johansan-Berg

We stand near the place of new birth.
Let us shine with the light of your love.

We turn from the crib to the cross.
Let us shine with the light of your love.

We go to carry his light.
Let us shine with the light of your love.

Thanks be to God.

Common Worship: Times and Seasons

INDEX OF FIRST LINES

A green Shoot will sprout from Jesse's stump, 26

Almighty God, give us grace that we may cast away the works of darkness, 2

Almighty God, you have given us your only-begotten Son, 42

And the Word became flesh and lived among us, 38

And thou, Jesus, sweet Lord, 23

At Cana's wedding, long ago, 82

At the setting of the sun, 12

Be thou a bright flame before me, 74

Beckoning God, 76

Birth by drowning, 81

Blessed art thou, 52

Born in the night, 53

Christ is the morning star, 28

Christians, awake! salute the happy morn, 42

Come on, ye faithful, 65

Come, thou long-expected Jesus, 29

Cradled in the mystery, 37

Creator God, 78

Creator of the heavens, 73

Eternal God, 32

For everyone born, a place at the table, 62
For the darkness of waiting, 9
From the very first day we were there, taking it all in, 60

Glorious and forgiving king of heaven, 46
God of Abraham and Sarah, 4
God of grace, 57
God of hope, 55
God of the watching ones, 14
God, of your goodness, 36
God our Father, you gave to Zechariah and Elizabeth in their old age, 13
God our Father, you sent your Son full of grace and truth, 58
God our Father, you spoke to the prophets of old, 7
God our redeemer, 21
God, when I see how kings and nations, 74
Gracious Father, 59

Hark! the herald angels sing, 43
Heavenly Father, you have created a universe of light, 5
Help me to go forward, 72
Helpless God as child and crucified, 53
How silently, how silently, 32

I am no longer my own but yours, 68
I danced in the morning, 45

I never, O God, 24
I open the stable door, 48
I said to the man who stood, 67
In my mother's womb, 52
In the beginning was the Word, 42
In the silence before time began, 23

Jesus, good above all other, 50
Jesus, who came to earth as a helpless baby, 18

Let all mortal flesh keep silence, 33
Light looked down and beheld Darkness, 38
Little Lamb, who made thee, 49
Lo, he comes with clouds descending, 3
Lord, by the song of the angels, 75
Lord, I turn my thoughts, 6
Lord, it is night, 15
Lord Jesus Christ, your birth at Bethlehem, 34
Lord Jesus Christ, your world awaits you, 11
Lord Jesus, light of the world, 17
Lord, there is much in my mind that has healed, 56
Lord, we have sung these carols and heard this story, 30
Loving God, calling your friends in new and unexpected ways, 22
Loving God, we give you thanks for the shepherds in the fields, 43

Mary the slumdweller, 22
May God the Holy Spirit, 82
May the light of God illumine your path, 84

Nativity Child, 50

O come, O come, Emmanuel, and ransom captive Israel, 25
O come, O come, Emmanuel, God-with-us here and now to dwell, 29
O come, O come, thou David's key, 27
O eternal Light, 19
O God the Son, highest and holiest, 44
O Lord of Israel, ruler of your ancient people, 26
O Lord of light and salvation, 80
O Wisdom, coming forth from the Most High, 26
O worship the Lord in the beauty of holiness, 74
Of the Father's heart begotten, 47
Our heavenly Father, 4

Silent night, holy night, 34
Since you so graciously invite us, 35
Sing high, 64
Songs of thankfulness and praise, 83
Stirring the easy slumbers, 79
Stop, my child, 16

Thank you, 63
The kings, Lord, 78

The night is far spent, and the day is at hand, 11
The wise men were not wise because they wore big hats, 77
Thy kingdom come, O God, 28
Today, O God, 36
Too many people around me, Lord, 69

We are brighter than a thousand suns, 8
We pray for the coming of God's kingdom, 69
We stand near the place of new birth, 84
Welcome all wonders in one sight, 33
What can we bring to your sufficiency but our poverty, 35
Whatever is happening in this world, Lord, 71
When they saw that the star had stopped, 73
Who is this, whose human birth, 34
Why, God, 61
Will you come and see the light from the stable door, 75
With love and compassion, 8

Yea, Lord, we greet thee, 39
You keep us waiting, 5

INDEX OF AUTHORS AND SOURCES

Adam, David, 48
Ainger, Geoffrey, 53
Alcuin, 19
Anselm, 23
Ashwin, Angela, 26

Bede, The Venerable, 28
Bible, Authorized Version (AV), 11
Bible, The Message, 27, 60
Bible, New Revised Standard Version (NRSV), 38, 42, 73
Blake, William, 49
Book of Common Order of the Church of Scotland 11, 36
Book of Common Prayer, The, 2
Brooks, Phillips, 32
Byrom, John, 42

Calvin, John, 35, 71
Carter, Sydney, 45
Cennick, John, 3
Cloth for the Cradle, 14
Colquhoun, Frank, 4
Columba of Iona, St, 74

Common Worship, 21, 59
Common Worship: Times and Seasons, 4, 5, 7, 8, 13, 17, 32, 42, 44, 58, 68, 73, 75, 78, 82, 84
Compston, Kate, 35, 63, 76
Cotter, Jim, 22, 27, 29

Dearmer, Percy, 50
Dudley-Smith, Timothy, 34, 82
Dunstan, St, 46

Goodland, Patrick, 18
Griffiths, Angela, 18

Hardwick, Susan, 61
Haskins, Minnie Louise, 67
Hensley, Lewis, 28
Housman, Laurence, 38

Iona Community Worship Book, 5

Johansan-Berg, John, 43, 84
Julian of Norwich, 36, 43

King, Dermot, SJ, 77

Lewin, Ann, 65, 81
Liturgy of St James, 33

Marsh, Pat, 6, 16, 37, 51, 79
Mohr, Joseph, 34
Monsell, John Samuel Bewley, 74
Morley, Janet, 10
Moultrie, Gerard, 33
Murray, Shirley Erena, 62

Neale, John Mason, 25, 47
Neary, Donal, SJ, 77
New Patterns for Worship, 69
Newell, J. Philip, 12, 23, 52
Noticias Aliadis, 22

Oakeley, Frederick, 39

Patrick, Johnstone G., 64
Perry, Michael, 18
Peterson, Eugene H., 24, 69, 74
Promise of His Glory, The, 26
Prudentius, 47

Quoist, Michel, 72

Scott, Janice, 78
Searle, John, 30
Sheppard, David, 80

Taylor, Michael H., 53

Vows and Partings, 15, 55, 56, 57

Warwicker, Bob, 8
Wesley, Charles,3, 29, 43
Wordsworth, Christopher, 83
Worlock, Derek, 80
Wren, Brian, 75

Young, John F., 34

ACKNOWLEDGEMENTS

The compiler and publisher gratefully acknowledge permission to reproduce copyright material in this anthology. Every effort has been made to trace and contact copyright holders. If there are any inadvertent omissions we apologize to those concerned; please send any information to the publisher who will make a full acknowledgement in future editions.

Scripture taken from THE MESSAGE is copyright © 1993, 1994, 1995, 1996, 2000, 2001, 2002. Used by permission of NavPress Publishing Group.

Scripture quotations from the New Revised Standard Version of the Bible (NRSV) are copyright © by the National Churches of Christ in the USA. Used by permission. All rights reserved.

Extracts from *The Book of Common Prayer* (1662) the rights in which are vested in the Crown are reproduced by permission of the Crown's Patentee, Cambridge University Press.

The Archbishops' Council of the Church of England: *Common Worship: Services and Prayers for the Church of*

England (2000) (pp. 21, 59); *Common Worship: Times and Seasons* (2006) (pp. 4, 5, 7, 8, 13, 17, 32, 34, 42, 44, 58, 68, 73, 75, 84); *New Patterns for Worship* (2003); *The Promise of His Glory* (1990) (p. 26), all of which are copyright © the Archbishops' Council.

Cairns Publications: from Jim Cotter, *Prayer in the Morning* (p. 22) and *Expectant Verses for Advent* (pp. 27, 29), copyright © Jim Cotter, 1989 and 2002.

Canterbury Press: from Philip J. Newell, *Sounds of the Eternal* (pp. 12, 23, 52) and Bob Warwicker, *Wisdom is Calling* (p. 8), copyright © Canterbury Press and imprint of Hymns Ancient and Modern. Used by permission.

Christian Education: from 'Mary the Slumdweller' by Noticias Aliades (p. 22).

Church of Scotland, Worship and Doctrine, Mission and Discipleship Council: from *The Book of Common Order of the Church of Scotland*, 1994 (pp. 11, 36).

Church Pastoral Aid Society: from Dick Williams (ed.), *Prayers for Today's Church* (pp. 78, 80) and *More Prayers for Today's Church* (p. 30), used by permission.

ACKNOWLEDGEMENTS

The Columba Press: from Donald Neary SJ, *Praying in Advent*, 1987 (p. 77).

Epworth Press: from John Johansen-Berg, *Prayers of the Way*, 1992 (pp. 43, 84).

Gill and Macmillan: from Michel Quoist, *Pathways in Prayer*, copyright © 1989 (p. 72).

HarperCollins: from Eugene H. Peterson, *Praying with Jesus*, 1993 (pp. 24, 69, 74) and Michael Perry (ed.), *Prayers for the People*, 1992 (p. 18).

Hodder: from Frank Colquhoun, *Contemporary Parish Prayers*, 1975 (p. 4).

Hope Publishing Company: from Shirley Erena Murray, 'From Everyone Born', copyright © Hope Publishing Co., Carol Stream, IL 60188 USA. All rights reserved. Used by permission (p. 62).

Ann Lewin: from 'Baptism' (p. 81) and 'Christmas Card' (p. 65) in *Waiting for the Kingfisher*, Canterbury Press, new edition 2009.

Pat Marsh: from 'Less than a Whisper Away' (p. 16),

'This Holy Ground' (p. 37 'Nativity Child' (p. 51), 'Not and Easy Option' (p. 79) from *Whispers of Love*, Foundery Press, copyright © Pat Marsh, 2003.

Kevin Mayhew Ltd: from 'Why God', copyright © Susan Hardwick, 1997, reproduced by permission of Kevin Mayhew Ltd (www.kevinmayhew.com). Licence nr 007082/2 (p. 61).

The Methodist Church: from *Vows and Partings*, copyright © Trustees for Methodist Church Purposes. Used with permission of Methodist Publishing (pp. 15, 55, 56, 57).

Oxford University Press: from the hymns 'Where do Christian songs begin?' (p. 34) and 'At Cana 's wedding long ago' (p. 82) by Timothy Dudley Smith (b. 1926), copyright © Timothy Dudley Smith in Europe and Africa, copyright © Hope Publishing Company in the United States of America and the rest of the world. Reproduced by permission of Oxford University Press. All rights reserved.

SPCK: from David Adam, *The Open Gate*, 2006 (p. 48) and Janet Morley (ed.), *Bread of Tomorrow*, 1992 (pp. 10, 35, 53, 63, 76).

Stainer and Bell: from Sydney Carter, 'Lord of the Dance', copyright © 1963 (p. 45), Geoffrey Ainger, 'Born in the Night', copyright © 1964 (p. 54) and Brian Wren, 'Will you come and see the light?', copyright © 1993 (p. 75), Stainer & Bell Ltd, London, England, www.stainer.co.uk.

Wild Goose Resource Group: from 'You keep us waiting', *The Iona Community Worship Book* (p. 5) and *Cloth for the Cradle*, 'God of the watching ones' text by John Bell (p. 14), Wild Goose Publications, 1997, copyright © 1997, WGRG, Iona Community, Glasgow G2 3DH, Scotland; www.wgrg.co.uk.